TABLE OF CONTENTS

BEAST OF THE ROAD

The Nissan GT-R is about to take off.
The driver inside buzzes with excitement.
He wants to see what this speedy **supercar**
is made of!

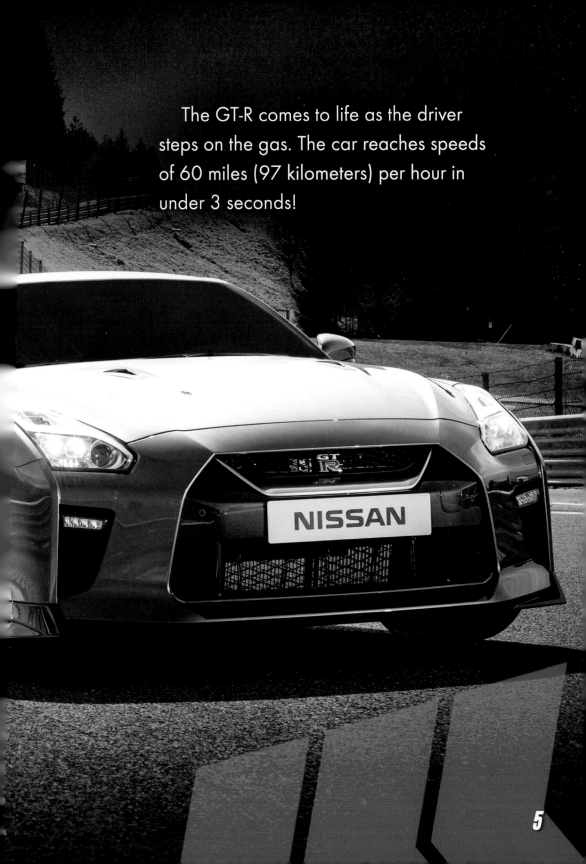

The GT-R comes to life as the driver steps on the gas. The car reaches speeds of 60 miles (97 kilometers) per hour in under 3 seconds!

The powerful GT-R rounds corners with ease. Its engine roars as it speeds faster down a straight stretch of pavement.

The GT-R is always a thrilling ride.
Nissan's supercar is a beast of the road!

THE HISTORY OF NISSAN

Nissan is one of the largest carmakers in the world. It began in 1911 as Kwaishinsha Motor Car Works. The brand was one of Japan's first large car companies. Its first **model**, the DAT, came out in 1914.

1914 Kwaishinsha DAT

THE NISSAN CEDRIC SPECIAL MODEL HAD A TALL TASK IN 1964. THE CAR WAS CHOSEN TO CARRY THE TORCH IN THAT YEAR'S OLYMPIC GAMES!

1963 Nissan Cedric

Kwaishinsha Motor Car Works combined with several other car companies in the 1930s. Its name was soon changed to Nissan.

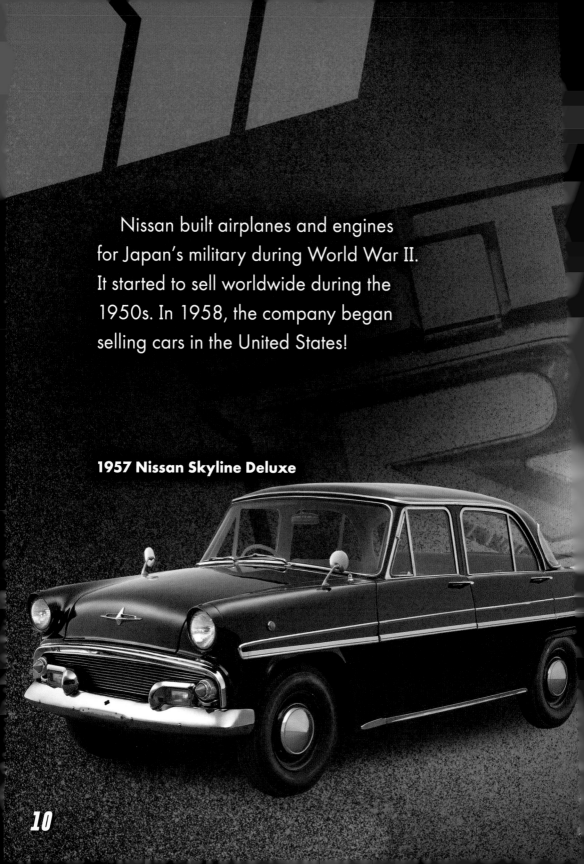

Nissan built airplanes and engines for Japan's military during World War II. It started to sell worldwide during the 1950s. In 1958, the company began selling cars in the United States!

1957 Nissan Skyline Deluxe

TOP OF THE WORLD

THE NISSAN LEAF IS THE WORLD'S BEST-SELLING ELECTRIC CAR. IT WON THE AWARD FOR WORLD CAR OF THE YEAR AT THE 2011 NEW YORK AUTO SHOW!

2018 Nissan Leaf

Today, Nissan is known for its safe cars. It even makes **electric cars**! The company also owns the Mitsubishi brand.

NISSAN GT-R

GT-R models have been around since 1969. The Skyline GT-R is one of the fastest race cars in Japanese history. It won every event it raced in for four straight years!

1969 Skyline 2000 GT-R

THE ROBOT SUPERCAR

NISSAN BUILT THE GT-R TO HONOR JAPANESE ART. THE CAR'S BODY WAS MADE TO LOOK LIKE THE CARTOON ROBOT GUNDAM!

NISSAN

**Nissan GT-R concept car
2001 Tokyo Motor Show**

The GT-R's current **generation** started as a **concept car** at the 2001 Tokyo Motor Show. But Nissan took its time finishing its perfect supercar. The GT-R was not sold until 2007.

TECHNOLOGY AND GEAR

suspension system

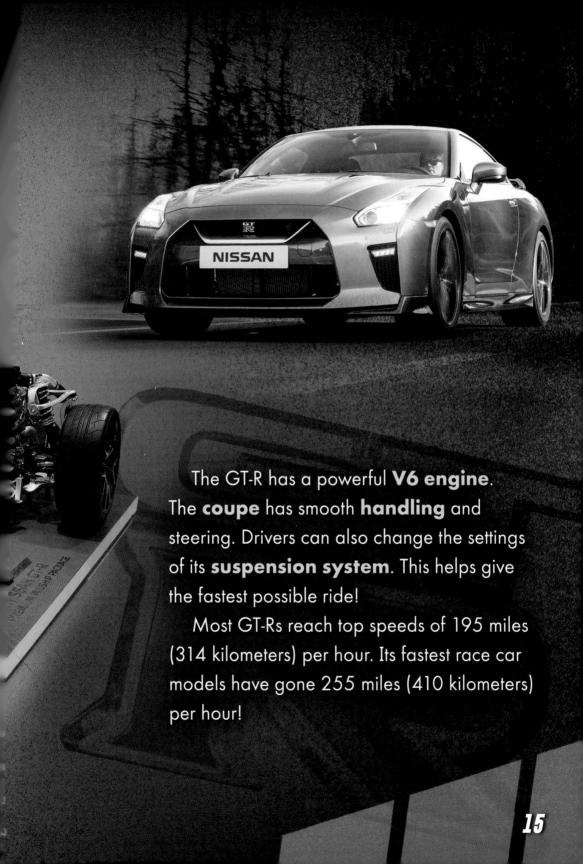

The GT-R has a powerful **V6 engine**. The **coupe** has smooth **handling** and steering. Drivers can also change the settings of its **suspension system**. This helps give the fastest possible ride!

Most GT-Rs reach top speeds of 195 miles (314 kilometers) per hour. Its fastest race car models have gone 255 miles (410 kilometers) per hour!

The GT-R's body was built to be bold and strong. A wide grille helps keep the engine cool. The car's hood is also extra sturdy. This keeps it from denting at high speeds.

grille

side skirt

rear diffuser

The GTR's **rear diffuser** makes the car extra **aerodynamic**. Long **side skirts** direct air around the car to give it the smoothest ride.

Inside, expensive leather covers the GTR's dashboard and seats. An 8-inch (20-centimeter) touch screen comes with **GPS navigation**.

Eleven speakers keep sound crystal clear inside the GT-R! The car's windshield has special glass to keep wind and road noise outside the car.

touch screen

2019 NISSAN GT-R SPECIFICATIONS

CAR STYLE	COUPE
ENGINE	3.8L V6
TOP SPEED	195 MILES (315 KILOMETERS) PER HOUR
0 - 60 TIME	2.7 SECONDS
HORSEPOWER	565 HP (421 KILOWATTS) @ 6,800 RPM
CURB WEIGHT	3,929 POUNDS (1,782 KILOGRAMS)
WIDTH	74.6 INCHES (190 CENTIMETERS)
LENGTH	185.4 INCHES (471 CENTIMETERS)
HEIGHT	53.9 INCHES (137 CENTIMETERS)
WHEEL SIZE	20 INCHES (51 CENTIMETERS)
COST	STARTS AT $99,990

TODAY AND THE FUTURE

Nissan has said the next model of the GT-R will be the fastest sports car in the world. It may run on both gas and electricity! But Nissan will not release the new GT-R until the early 2020s.

The next model will have giant shoes to fill. The Nissan GT-R is an amazing supercar!

WIDE GRILLE

LONG SIDE SKIRTS

REAR DIFFUSER

FAST AND FURIOUS

THE NISSAN GT-R HAS BEEN SEEN ON MOVIE SCREENS SEVERAL TIMES. BRIAN O'CONNER DROVE THE CAR IN THE FAST AND THE FURIOUS SERIES!

GLOSSARY

aerodynamic—having a shape that can move through the air quickly

concept car—a car made to highlight new styles or technology; concept cars are not usually for sale.

coupe—a car with a hard roof and two doors

electric cars—cars powered completely by electricity

generation—a version of a model

GPS navigation—a car system that provides maps and directions to get around

handling—how a car performs around turns

model—a specific kind of car

rear diffuser—a part on the back underside of a car that directs air and makes the car more aerodynamic

side skirts—lips on the bottom sides of a car's body that make the car more aerodynamic

supercar—an expensive and high-performing sports car

suspension system—a series of springs and shocks that help a car grip the road

V6 engine—an engine with 6 cylinders arranged in the shape of a "V"

Are you ready to take it to the extreme?
Torque books thrust you into the action-packed world
of sports, vehicles, mystery, and adventure. These books
may include dirt, smoke, fire, and dangerous stunts.
WARNING: read at your own risk.

This edition first published in 2020 by Bellwether Media, Inc.

No part of this publication may be reproduced in whole or in part without written permission of the publisher.
For information regarding permission, write to Bellwether Media, Inc., Attention: Permissions Department,
6012 Blue Circle Drive, Minnetonka, MN 55343.

Library of Congress Cataloging-in-Publication Data

Names: Sommer, Nathan, author.
Title: Nissan GT-R / by Nathan Sommer.
Description: Minneapolis, MN : Bellwether Media, Inc., [2020] | Series:
   Torque. Car Crazy | Includes bibliographical references and index. |
   Audience: Age 7-12.
Identifiers: LCCN 2018061013 (print) | LCCN 2019000281 (ebook) | ISBN
   9781618915528 (ebook) | ISBN 9781644870112 (hardcover : alk. paper)
Subjects: LCSH: Nissan GT-R automobile–Juvenile literature.
Classification: LCC TL215.N54 (ebook) | LCC TL215.N54 S66 2020 (print) | DDC
   629.222/2–dc23
LC record available at https://lccn.loc.gov/2018061013

Editor: Kate Moening   Designer: Josh Brink

Printed in the United States of America, North Mankato, MN.

NISSAN
GT-R

BY NATHAN SOMMER

BELLWETHER MEDIA • MINNEAPOLIS, MN

TO LEARN MORE

AT THE LIBRARY

Adamson, Thomas K. *Sports Cars*. Minneapolis, Minn.: Bellwether Media, 2019.

Farndon, John. *Megafast Cars*. Minneapolis, Minn.: Hungry Tomato, 2016.

McCollum, Sean. *The World's Fastest Cars*. North Mankato, Minn.: Capstone Press, 2017.

ON THE WEB

FACTSURFER

Factsurfer.com gives you a safe, fun way to find more information.

1. Go to www.factsurfer.com.

2. Enter "Nissan GT-R" into the search box and click 🔍.

3. Select your book cover to see a list of related web sites.

INDEX

The images in this book are reproduced through the courtesy of: Grzegorz Czapski, front cover; Nissan Press Room, pp. 4-5, 6-7, 10, 12 (top), 15, 16, 17, 18, 19, 20-21, 21 (top left, top middle, top right). Datsun, p. 8; sv1ambo, p. 9; FeelGoodLuck, p. 11; Kurita KAKU/ Getty, p. 13; Kazick, p. 14.